W9-BAM-325

RULES OF ENGAGEMENT

RULES OF ENGAGEMENT
100 pages for the single man

A Book by Diesel

Diesel Media and Publication
Los Angeles

A DIESEL MEDIA AND PUBLICATION ORIGINAL, MAY 2005

Rules of Engagement
100 Pages for the Single Man
First Edition

Illustrations are work-for-hire by Wayne Cash
of Wayne-Dre Studios.
www.waydre.deviantart.com

Manufactured in the United States of America.

ISBN 0-9768600-0-7

www.roelife.com

Pre-Season

So how many days do I wait to call her after a first date? Should I or should I not buy a drink for that cute girl at the bar? These questions and many others like them are why men struggle with dating. The reason, there is no right answer! Some men claim they know; and we have seen countless movies, but trust me, they're wrong! Every situation is different and the only way to know the right answer is to understand the game, or what I call: **Rules of Engagement**.

Yes…like any other sport, dating is a game. And like any game, it has rules. No matter how hard we try to avoid playing, it's inevitably something we all do. The real question is, how well do you play and how can you improve? That's where this book comes in.

This book analyzes the fundamental rules of play and help you better understand the game. It uses sports analogies to illustrate answers to questions you've always dreamed of knowing. Don't be a fool, no matter how good you think you know the game, no one can win every time. But there are a number of things you can do to better your odds.

This book is different than other books because it gives positive advice on how to win in the game of dating while having fun along the way. It will build your friendships, confidence and change your social life!

Consider this book a coach's playbook to his players. It has good advice and plays that work in all kinds of situations. There are even a few plays for your special teams (your wingmen). These plays, when practiced and well executed, have a high percentage of helping you perform better while on the dating field. Learn them, use them, and adapt them to become the ultimate dating athlete!

Most of the book's intentions are to be positive and informative, but there are occasional times that I get a bit harsh. Like any good coach, it's necessary and it's only constructive criticism. Nevertheless, whether offended or enlightened, by its end, you will have learned many useful tips and be ready for "game time."

Table of Contents

The Locker Room

First, let's establish that when it comes to dating, women are kicking our asses! If dating were a football game, they'd be winning 42-7. We're losing because we neglect the fundamental rules, and our team, which includes all males, is playing sloppy. Easily avoidable mistakes and early fumbles are ruining it for everyone. Women see us as predictable and easy tackles. Consider this halftime and I want to introduce you to a new playbook for the second half.

Now, before we go and charge the field, let's analyze our first half. When looked at on a broad scale, dating for you is similar to dating for the next guy. We all have brilliant opportunities, so how we handle the ball makes the difference between winning and losing. Just by buying this book, you have a head start because it means you're willing to practice. This excludes you from the "I'm too good to practice" mentality some arrogant players have and don't realize, no one's above

1

the game.

Moving on, let me analyze our team and illustrate how we've been playing sloppy. You must be wondering, "how do a bunch of random guys at a bar qualify as my teammates? I don't even know them!"

Good question…take for example this common scenario:

While recently at a bar, I started surveying the scene and noticed a whole bunch of random guys hovering around waiting for girls to show up. It felt like a bunch of players on the sidelines stretching before a game. Eventually, girls started showing up and every five feet or so another guy would jump in front with some sort of pickup line. It almost felt as though it was a race, and they needed to sprint off the line to win. I call these guys "Snappers" because at first crack, they're out the gates. Not only are Snappers annoying, they also give the other team an early overconfident advantage. Nevertheless, no major harm has been done and Snappers are only a fraction of the larger problem. Alcohol then comes into play! Now with the right player, this is usually not a problem, but some players shift from pickup lines to grabbing asses. One thing I can guarantee is that girls hate being a piece of meat, and any type of random groping puts them on the defensive. Soon the girls moved to the dance floor and what I call "Vulture Syndrome" occurs. Girls are dancing in the center while random guys circle around waiting for a look or opportunity to jump in. At this point, our drunk teammates start getting desperate and do dumb things. For example, I saw a guy grab an opposing player's ponytail to get her attention. As you can imagine, she was not only unhappy, she was also disgusted and I could literally see her attitude about the night change. So now, by the time I got around to talking to a girl I thought was attractive, she had already been "hit on" ten times, had her ass grabbed twice, and her hair had been pulled. She was now officially "on the defensive" and it was only 10:30 p.m. She wanted nothing to do with anyone but her friends and/or any guys she came with. Thus, our teammates (other random guys) have ruined the game for everyone. When you have a bunch of defensive girls, it spreads like the plague and soon no one is getting any love!

I know this sounds condescending, but I just want to illustrate how our actions make women react the opposite way we intend. Unfortunately, this behavior will never go away. It would be like changing the wind to get men in general to act different. So, if you want to be better than the average guy, you must compensate by making a few adjustments to the way you play. With that said, let's now look at the other team and how they play different.

When it comes to women, men tend to judge looks over anything else. Shallow as this may seem, it's the undeniable truth. If she's "smoking hot," other qualities take a back seat and are not an issue. In the long run, this mentality will be the end of you because a girl never wants to be a piece of meat. If you're ever going to succeed, you must expand your criteria to more that just physical appearance. Women on the other hand, search for a whole different set of standards. Better known as the four "S": Sexy, Sense of Humor, Sensitivity, and Success! As you can see, we have it much harder, and that is where we begin. I call it the "Dating Rat Race," and in today's match up, we have the cats chasing the mice and mice chasing the cheese. I want you to be the cheese!

Who am I and why am I qualified to give you advice and strategies for dating in the 21st century?

Good question…I don't consider myself a guru in dating. I'm just a guy who's been paying attention and wrote all this shit down. There is no magic play that make automatic touchdowns, but there are circumstances that when recognized can be converted into possible yardage for your side.

I don't always win, and no...I can't go out there and score every time. But, I have played the game long enough to jot down some good plays that will help you on the field. I've also done some calculations on my spending and have realized the following scary conclusion.

There are 52 weeks in the year. My friends and I go out between 2 and 4 times a week, which is an average of 156 times a year. I spend roughly $60-80 dollars per outing and given my 7-year run, I currently sit at 1092 bars and clubs with a shocking $70,980.00 dollar bar tab. Even more shocking is my friends have spent equally as much doing the very same thing. No matter how you look at it, that's quite an education! Yet, bars and spending money are not the emphasis of this book. I consider this book a coach's guidelines to the single life. It's a compilation of ideas and techniques accumulated over time. Although you may not agree with the theories disclosed, it doesn't hurt to review and compare these techniques with your own experiences. For those of you already comfortable in the scene, this material may be familiar and help reinforce your existing skills. For others, this book will teach you the fundamental rules of the game and provide you countless hours of laughs with your friends.

Why did I decide to write this book?

Another good question...I, like most of you, constantly find myself challenged by dating obstacles. Although I've had some amazing experiences, I've also had some tough defeats. This is the most complicated game in life to play, and we face savvy and slippery competitors. They are cunning, patient, and have less desire than we do to score.

I wrote this book because I see guys around me making mistakes, fumbling the ball, and generally just hurting the team. It's my goal to share experiences and provide examples that have been effective on the field. The best part is that my references are entertaining and comical, so this book will be a breeze to read. In conversation, I have always heard my friends say, "Someone should write a book on this shit." Well boys "here's the shit, Enjoy!"

How will "the shit" help me?

Each defeat helps us adapt and adjust to the other team. I find myself in predictable and recurring situations and capitalize on past experiences in order to pull out a win. I also find myself constantly giving advice and strategies to many of my friends.

Worst case, this book will create one or more successful

plays and provide countless hours of laughs. More likely, you will be educated on dating mistakes and in turn, make better decisions on future opportunities.

So, if you're ready, let's huddle up and talk about our drive down the field.

The 20

In The Huddle

In any game, especially this one, it is very important to prepare yourself physically and mentally. Recently, my brother surprised me with the perfect analogy, "Getting a hot girl is like fishing, you have to be in the right place, at the right time, with the right bait." Translation, it's all about the right location, good timing, and most of all, you need your bait (YOU) ready!

I've broken this chapter into two aspects of the game. The first aspect is your physical strength and endurance; the second and important aspect is your mental abilities.

Let's start with the physical game.

Just like us, women admire a good body. Think of it this way, we, as men, are attracted to women who have a kick-ass body. Why would it be any different for them? I will go on the record and say, "Yes, a hot body will TURN ON women!" Abs, arms, chest, even calves, women each have their favorites. The only major difference between us and them is the x-factor. Women look for things like a good sense of humor equally as important as the body. Nevertheless, having a good body only increases your chances.

If you don't have a good body, don't despair. Do your best to get that butt in shape and focus on your personality; chances are it's your strong point anyways!

I recently lost forty pounds and you wouldn't believe the social change I've seen. Part of it is my own renewed self-confidence, but the weight lost has definitely increased my physical potential.

All in all, get a workout partner, go to the gym and eat right. If you want to better your social life, this is a great place to start.

Now...are you mentally ready?

Like I stated earlier, the mental game is equally, if not, more important than the physical game. I surveyed 100 women on what they look for in men. Ding, Ding, Ding, survey says...SELF-CONFIDENCE was on the top of the list. This means, if you have a low self-esteem because you just broke up with your "X" or haven't scored in a while, leave it on the bench!

Our man in *Swingers* the movie only got lucky in the end. That normally doesn't happen.

Another mental NO-NO is the "Pity Technique." This means that you're the guy who talks about his bad love life or recent breakup as a topic of regular conversation. For some reason, this one gets used a lot, and although it seems like you're winning her sympathy vote, what you don't know is that your chances with her are about as good as Shaq making a free throw. First reason, a girl doesn't want to hurt you, AGAIN! Better reason, you're not that self-confident man…and as you can guess, "weenie-ass-baby" didn't top my survey.

> *"I had a friend that used to always tell his dates about how sad he was about being dumped. Besides looking undesirable, he never scored once with this tactic, so I told him to throw it out of the playbook. His win/lose ratio has been much better since then."*

What should I do instead?
Instead, focus on the positives in your life! While you're at it, learn a few jokes, they always come in handy. A good sense of humor was the second highest quality that women look for in men.

Also, don't stress out on little setbacks. Not every game is going to go your way. You shouldn't put all your eggs in one basket. I know you've heard that plenty of times and that's why it is true. Dating is like golf, if you put your entire hopes for a good score in one shot and miss, you risk mentally ruining your entire game. Focus on the entire 18 holes. Relax, have fun, and you'll have a better game!

The final mental advice I can give before game time is to try and make some money. Being "broke as a joke" is depressing to yourself and your dating lifestyle. AMBITION is another great quality and sub-consciously gives you a higher level of confidence. It's hard to "pimp it" over macaroni and cheese and a 1972 brown Ford Tempo. Trust me, I owned a Tempo once and it was tough!

Let's now learn about our opponents.

The 30

Know Your Opponent

We're now in the 21st century. Women are twice as independent and more inclined to be single than ever before. Therefore, we have plenty of opportunities. In the past, we have been stereotyped as non-committal, predictable, and often meat-headed. What women don't know is that we're all just looking for that perfect girl to take us out of the game. Just because we don't like a girl doesn't mean we're non-committal. It just means she's not the one.

A good offense is always predicated on a good defense. Let's imagine you were coaching a major sports team and you stumble across the other team's playbook. Would you take it?   Hell ya!

With that said, I've just happened to find this playbook lying around. Let's take a peek...

The Woman's Playbook

The best way to understand women is to picture yourself in their shoes. Imagine knowing that on any given night, you were going to get in the club for free, have fourteen guys stare at your boobs, eight of those guys offer you free drinks, listen to six cheesy pickup lines, get stabbed on the dance floor by drunk guys with no dick control, and best of all, round off the night spending less than $15 dollars. What do you think your mental disposition would be?

Just so you know, typically a women will...take the doorman's free in, avoid the perverts, turn down four of the eight drinks, throw out a fake smile to the cheesy one liners, pivot around the dance floor all night avoiding drunk dudes, and go home alone looking forward to sleeping in her incredibly comfortable bed.

As you can see, their whole idea of going out is much different than ours. Just this morning I heard a woman on the radio mocking men on how easy it is to get free drinks at a club. Unfortunately, we are to blame for creating this mess and more unfortunate... they know it! In their minds it's justifiable because we expect to get laid, but we don't always get laid. More importantly, girls shouldn't accept our freebies unless they are mildly interested. Do they think we are buying a round because we enjoy throwing our money away? Nevertheless, this will always happen

14

and it's just part of the game. The bigger problem we must worry about is that it subconsciously gives them the upper hand. One of my goals in this book is to try and get men in general to elevate the bar when we're out on the field. I have no problem buying drinks or spending money, but when a girl asks for a drink and then walks away, realize that you were a sucker. You should have enough experience and common sense to recognize these traps before they happen.

Now, don't get me wrong. I don't want to come down hard on men. Life is good. We pee standing up and if you have the money, it's fun as hell to spend it! I just want men to realize when they're getting played and make the proper adjustments. This extends way past just free drinks, it's the entire mentality of dating. Don't be a sucker and women won't treat you like one! Having what's commonly known as "Good Game" is the key to attracting women and is an important part of your social life.

Secondly, don't assume women are innocent. I see more and more girls cheating these days, and they're not any better for it. We usually have the bad rep for cheating, but the truth is, it's not a sex-related problem. Male or female, cheaters are "Cheaters." We all need to cut it out. If you've retired from the game, your days on the field are done. Get over it!

To conclude and refocus the purpose of this chapter, I will summarize: The main reason why it's harder for guys to hook up, is the general assumption that we need to hook up…which we do! But, we have to keep our game faces. We need to sub-consciously make our opponents believe that hooking up with us is a challenge. In the beginning, it's best to keep them guessing. Girls like the chase and love the challenge. The minute they smell defeat, consider the game over because you'll have a hard time gaining any yardage.

Therein lies the theory. So let's move on to the things that make it work! In the next set of chapters, I will take you through the top 10 rookie mistakes, lingo for you and your friends, best fields of play, the rules of the game, patented hand signals you can use on the field, and a few ways to pull out a win even when you think the game is over.

There's the coin toss, suit up and let's go!

The 40

Top 10 Rookie Mistakes

As an athlete, there are mistakes that can take you out of the game. Any good coach will tell you that a little jump on what not to do can be the difference between a win or a loss. With that said, here are the top 10 rookie mistakes to watch out for. They are in reverse order:

Number 10: Mr. Forgetful

"Come on man…try to remember the plays." If you've heard this one while playing street ball as a kid, you're probably losing some serious points with the ladies as well. You have to listen to what girls say if you want to run the bases. For example, a good way to throw the inning would be to forget the girl's name you've been talking to for the last forty minutes. A error this late could cost you the game, and it happens all the time. Nothing is more obvious than asking your friend to find out her name. Trust me, they know! Plus, "hey baby" or "hey sweetness" gets old and it's a dead giveaway that you're Mr. Forgetful. It basically tells her you're too dumb to remember her name and guess what…that translates into her perception of your play. Here's the trick…when you shake hands for the first time, listen to her name and say it three times in your head. Rule of thumb, only do this for the ones you really like or you'll drive yourself crazy trying to remember everybody.

Don't think you're in the clear just by remembering a name. You also need to pay attention to your general conversation skills as well. Try to not ask her the same damn questions over and over again. "Where do you work again?" is annoying and makes you once more look like Mr. Forgetful. If you're a bad listener, you'll definitely need to work this out.

Number 9: Mr. Ugly Shoes
Good fashion is important! One area men always seem to forget is the shoes!

> *"No…Socks with sandals will never be cool!"*
> -Diesel

Would you believe that some guys think that one pair of tennis shoes are enough for every situation? That's not you, right?

Girls notice you from head to toe. Please, my brother, pick up a copy of UNleashed™, FHM™ or Maxim™ and get to the shoe store. At minimum, a dress shoe, tennis shoe, and cool street shoe are required. If you're really lost, use your eyes and look around the floor for an hour and pick up a few trendy names from the dudes around you.

Number 8: Mr. Conservative

Sure we all get nervous! That's what lets us know we're into someone. Yet playing Mr. Conservative and not loosening up will get you nowhere. If she wants to dance, and you're a horrible dancer, sack up and get out there! Even though you suck, she will think it's cute that you tried to still have fun. It's better to have taken a risk and get out there than to just sit on the bench. It's hard to win a game from the sidelines.

Number 7: Mr. Head on a Swivel

There is nothing worse than a man who can't keep his eye on the ball. When you're on a first or second date, try to keep your A.D.D. mind on the girl you're with. When you're staring at "SportsCenter" on the bar TV or checking out other girls, your date noticed. A few more of those and she'll call the game on account of rain.

Number 6: Mr. Touchy-Feely in Public

Do you know what happens when you don't give a small flame enough oxygen? It goes out! Just like the little flame, in the beginning, smothering can steal the oxygen in a relationship.

Instead, play a good defense and let her run her offense. There is nothing wrong with some subtle hints to let her know you like her, but make those actions small. Try little things like guiding her through the door and touching the small of her back. Avoid major moves like petting her head or grabbing her ass, those are relationship kinds of stuff.

Number 5: Mr. Arrogant

Good news, there are a handful of girls that find you sexy. Unfortunately, most find you arrogant! Girls may find the arrogant guy attractive at first, but it quickly wears off. Tone it down a notch and you will be a stud.

Number 4: Mr. Call Too Much

The worst thing you can do in a new relationship is be over-anxious. You have an entire lifetime to get to know a girl, calling her three times in a row is not necessary. I know you're excited, but like fish, girls get spooked easily. The better looking they are, the spookier they become. Call her once and wait for her to call you back. If she doesn't, you have to bite the bullet and understand that she may just not be into you. Nothing's worse than getting "the talk" stating how sorry she is and that she doesn't feel it.

Here is the best rule of thumb. Call once, if you get her voice mail, leave a short, non-babbling message. Then wait! If she likes you, she will call, I promise. If she doesn't call, you need to wait at least four to five days. Then you can try only one more time. After a second message with no call back, that's it, you're finished. Don't run this track anymore; you never get good lap times!

Number 3: Mr. Dragon Breath

One of the biggest turn-offs for a women is a man with kickin' ass breath. Officially known as halitosis, once you're marked with this problem, you're marked for life! Get some mints, especially on the early dates, and avoid eating onions or garlic. It's not worth the potential risk! Secondly, use a toothpick to keep those teeth alligator free. An alligator is when you have a poppy-seed or piece of food stuck between your teeth. There's no reason to be A.G.L. (defined later) with things you could be easily fixing.

Number 2: Mr. Speed Talker

Before going out on a first date, I would avoid the ephedrine, speed or Red Bulls. Racing out words makes you look insecure and immature. Last time I checked, girls didn't describe the perfect guy as tall, dark and hyper!

The Number 1 Rookie Mistake:
Mr. Over Compliment

We all know that complimenting a woman is important and necessary, but few know that over-complimenting can kill you.

For some reason, when you over-compliment, a woman tends to assume you're hooked and considers the challenge gone. People, in general, are funny about challenges. We all strive to climb bigger mountains; you don't see a whole bunch of people signing up to conquer hills.

I don't want this to be misunderstood. All I'm saying is, wait for a proper opportunity to compliment, and make sure you really mean it. Be careful not to use compliments that women find common. "I love your hair," has been used and used and doesn't say much for your originality. Weak compliments tend to hurt more than they help because you're saying the same thing she's heard tons of times before. If you can find a truly genuine compliment, it can be what wins the game, but inversely, the wrong compliment or too many compliments can lose credibility and may incur a penalty!

The 50

Lingo for You and the Boys

Aw yes…the art of communication! The ability to speak to your friends without the knowledge of your opponents is key to any game winning strategy. When to stay or when to leave, even when to call in re-enforcements can all be accomplished using lingo or hand signals. In a later chapter, I'll illustrate examples of effective hand signals. In this chapter, I focus on lingo.

Besides being an important part of any professional team, when applied to a social environment, with a tight group of friends, lingo can be extremely fun and entertaining! To get you started, I have outlined thirty-three terms. Feel free to use, modify, or create similar terms for yourself.

A.G.L. – Meaning "Anti-Get-Laid."

There are many uses of the term A.G.L. Most of the time it's used to tell a friend there's something wrong with his appearance, so he can then correct. Other times it can be used to describe a friend or tell him to go home.

Used in a sentence, "Hey bro, you're drunk and A.G.L., go home!"

Another example:
"Hey bro, that's an A.G.L. zit on your nose!"

MORTON – Referring to "Morton's Salt." (Also can be referred to as "Salting.")

You're in a conversation with a beautiful woman and a friend walks over and starts ragging on you. That's considered throwing "salt" in your game. To let him know, call him **Morton**. He should "get it" and walk away.

Used in a sentence, "Excuse me Cindy, have you met my friend **Morton**?"

Clipped – As in...cut off.

If a girl you're dating starts to bother you, she's **clipped**. This is a quick term to update your friends on a recent breakup.

P.D.A. – Public Display of Affections.
Nothing's worse than watching two people grope each other. Too much **P.D.A.** is bad!

D.S.L's – Dick Sucking Lips (Ladies hate this one.)
No, not the Internet, **D.S.L's** is a term used when a girl has perfect sweet lips. Sometimes makes a difference when defending yourself with the boys.

Used in a sentence, "Hey Diesel, how could you hook up with that girl?" I reply, "Hey, did you see her **D.S.L's?**"

Spinner – Perfect 5 foot 4, 102 pounds..."wet," girl.
A hot "little" girl you would like to spin on your… (use your imagination.) A term used to describe a girl to your friends that is petite and hot.

Used in a sentence, "Look at that chick, she is a total **spinner!**"

The Grenade – The Anchor!

This is the friend in the pack of girls that someone better talk to or the whole group is leaving. She is bored, not into the scene, and going to ruin it for everybody. It's usually the girl not getting attention from the group. Funny thing about girls is that they stick together. If one is going home, say sayonara to them all.

Used in a sentence, "Hey bro, my girl is hot and diggin' me, I need you to jump on the **grenade**!"

Smoking – A really hot girl.

Can be over used! Not every girl is smoking hot! Some are just hot. The best of the best are **smoking**.

Used in a sentence, "I was just talking to the hottest girl!"
  Your friend asks, "**smoking**?"
   You reply "**SMOKING!**"

Nails – A synonym to smoking.

A step down from smoking. This is another way to describe a hot girl.

Used in a sentence, "She had a tight body, she was **nails**!"

Wingman – Also known as wingmen or wingdawg.
This one should need little explaining, but it refers to your partners in crime…your boys!

Used in a sentence, "I need a **wingman** for those two girls!"

Textbook – The perfect execution.
This is how you describe a really good date! It's when every element of the date fell into place as if it were written in a textbook.

Used in a sentence, "Boys, my date with Sarah was **textbook**!"

Divide and Conquer
This is a valuable technique I cover in depth later. Basically it means to even the ratio of women to men in the group. An even ratio has a better percentage of everyone hooking up.

Used in a sentence, "Last night was a perfect example of a **divide and conquer** situation. Good job boys!"

Cross-eyed – Really Drunk!

This is when you get really drunk! So drunk you can't see straight.

Used in a sentence, "Hey man, after that shot of uncle jager last night, you were cross-eyed!"

Locked – A sure thing!

This is when a girl is really, really into you.

Used in a sentence, "Oh Lisa, she's **locked**!"

Shoe-laces-tied – Head-over-heels for someone.

Another term to describe a girl that is completely into you. When her shoe-laces are tied, it's a figure of speech to tell your friends she's falling for you.

Used in a sentence, "Diesel, What's up with that girl you dated last week?" I reply, **shoe-laces-tied**!"

Posterized – Stared down by a girl.

This is when a girl stares at you so long that you think to yourself, "Maybe I should just stop so she can take a good look!" Usually this is used after the alleged incident to update your friends.

Used in a sentence: "Hey guys, I was just **posterized**!"

Laminized – She stared so long you feel like you've been laminated and saved for later.

One degree higher than posterized, this is when she not only stared, but also gave you a seductive eye. In these situations, to not stop and followup would be foolish!

Used in a sentence, "Hey bro, I was just put on a poster and **laminized**, I'm going back!"

Schmeebs

The Perfect Boobs!

Every once in a while a great term gets invented and just sticks. This is a great one I have to credit to my friend, Clark. "Good one Clark!" It's the best-hidden way to comment on perfect boobies without girls realizing it. It's so secret, you could say it right in front of them, and they won't get it.

For example, you and your buddy are standing in line at a fast food joint. A cute girl with a RACK is next to you. You say to your buddy, "**Schmeeeeeeebbs!**" - he looks!

Schlobbs
Big, but fatty boobs.

A fat chick with big boobs! Usually a term used to correct a friend's mistaken assessment of Schmeebs.

Used in a sentence, "C'mon, she's fat, those are **schlobbs!**"

Schlomachs – rhymes with stomach
Old saggy melons

These are saggy boobs that hang down toward to the stomach.

Used in a sentence, "Those aren't schlobbs, those are more like **schlomachs!**"

Schlankles – rhymes with ankles
Old porn star boobs.

The fourth degree of Clark's terminology refers to rarely seen, outrageously big and saggy boobs that sarcastically hang down towards the ankles.

Dibs – To claim first right to a girl.

When you're with your friends and you see a hot girl, you can call **dibs** on her. This means you get a half an hour window to work your magic until she's free game again. The purpose is to avoid four of your boys all chasing the same girl, which is never beneficial!

Important note: There are rules to calling **dibs** just as there's rules to calling "Shotgun." You can't always be the one calling **dibs** or your boys will get pissed off, so use it wisely!

Snaggle – A girl with bad teeth. (A.K.A. summer teeth – some of her teeth are here, summer there!)

This is when a girl is pretty, but when she smiles, her teeth are going every which direction.

Furuno™ – your girl radar!

In boating, a **Furuno™** is a brand of radar device that scans for other ships in the area. If your **Furuno™** is on, that means you're actively pinging the room for girls.

Used in a sentence, your friend says, "Hey, you see that hot girl way in the corner?" you reply, "Damn, you have your **Furuno™** on bro!"

Picked Off – she caught you staring dammit!

She came…you saw…and you stared! All the while she caught you doing it. This one applies to all kinds of examples but mainly it's when you have your whole body twisted around checking out a girl and she catches you doing it.

Used in a sentence, "Aww Shit, I just got **picked off**!!"

Swivel – constantly checking out girls!

If your head is on a **swivel**, this means you're constantly looking all around for girls. Usually a negative term used to tell a friend he's looking around to much.

Used in a sentence, "Hey bro, you head's on a freakin' **swivel** today, stop it! You're gonna get us **picked off**!"

Take away – a technique to change a girls mind about you.

The **take away** is a technique I go into in-depth later in the book. Basically it means you take away a constant (like calling her) in order to spark a response. This sometimes confuses girls, and may change the momentum of a losing game.

On-the-Gas – to be all over a girl!

If your friend is **on-the-gas**, he's trying too hard to get a girl. The next day you can comment, "Last night, you were **on-the-gas**, slow down or you'll lose her!"

Bogies – cute girls in the area!

This is how you notify the boys of a cute girl or girls in the area.

Used in a sentence, "Hey guys, **bogies** on my six!"

Pamplona – the running of the babes!

This is a good thing! This is when a bar decides to provide girls with a male stripper before they officially open. It's called **Pamplona** because when you get there, the girls are really aggressive and may charge you like bulls. This can also be used when describing a place that has a ratio of girls that's 2 to 1. In these scenarios, **Pamplona** may occur.

Cock-block-a-sauris-rex – the good ol' guy who ruins it for you!

This is the guy that always gets in the way of a good thing between you and a girl. Usually it occurs when you're at a bar while talking with a girl, when suddenly **cock-block-a-sauris-rex** comes up and tries to steal her from you. In these situations, don't be afraid to belt out the **cock-block-a-sauris-rex** yell (make it up).

Tag & Release – when a girl is too young!

Ok, you've met the hottest girl you've ever seen only to find out she's under age. It happens! In this case, you need to **tag & release**. Get her number and email then release her back into the wild. Hit her up when she's of age.

Ready Five – Be ready when I call you

There always comes a time when you're out and you meet a couple ladies and are too few in numbers to entertain them all. In this case, you should call in your re-enforcements. It's called **ready five** because usually you've asked your friend to be ready on the deck for your call to come dogfight.

Used in a sentence while talking to a friend, "I'm meeting a few girls after dinner, I need you on **ready five** if they want to go out!"

The 60

Best Fields of Play

Below is a list, with explanatory reasoning, of what I feel are the best fields of play. Keep in mind, this is one opinion to another, so there are circumstances where theory can be proven wrong. Although, if you're a gambling man, you know it's all about the percentages, and these are what I call high percentage locations.

1. **The House Party:**
   Most people would think a club would be at the top of the list. Would you believe that it's actually third? And that's only with special circumstances.

   The reality is, a house party dominates the list. Especially if you're throwing it and you have an exciting theme such as "Pimp's and Ho's" or "Anything for a Buck."

Yes, I know this seems fraternity-ish. But, parties are all about fun and whenever you have a mind-altering theme, it leads to mind-altering egos, which is directly related to mind-altering hooking up!

There are several other theoretical reasons why a house party is so successful. At a house party, girls are more comfortable and therefore drink more than they normally would at a club. Drinking leads to less defense and more offense, and that leads to your buddy's room.

Another great thing about house parties is you don't need to fork out a bunch of money to have a good time. The bar scene is always more expensive and the next day you always regret it! When throwing a party, always make sure you invite an even ratio and have plenty of liquid courage to last the night. Nothings worse than a dry party or sausagefest!

2. **Spring Break Vacation: which includes New Orleans, Vegas, Florida, The Bahamas, Hawaii, and anywhere in Mexico:**
When girls are on spring break, their alter I.D.G.A.F (I don't give a fuck!) egos come out. Mainly it's because they're with a group

of girls and looking to be crazy. Don't be fooled, girls love to get crazy! They just don't like to get too wild in their hometowns…but while outside state lines, it's ON!

3.

Club/bar with a pre-arranged group:

Like I said earlier, clubs didn't make it on the list, but when you bring your own sand to the beach, it's a different story. Clubs are tough because by the time eleven o'clock rolls around, other rookie guys have ruined it for a smooth guy like yourself. By this time, girls are running around the club avoiding drunk-dudes with no game.

But…going to a club with your own set of girls is great because by the time eleven o'clock rolls around, the girls will be running around looking for you. This is because they came with you and they trust you. If you're organizing the night, the best-case scenario would be to invite an even ratio of girls and guys. In these cases, mixed with alcohol, one can only imagine the possibilities.

4. **Weddings: (Someone you know. Don't crash one.)**

Like house parties, weddings are another place where girls feel extremely comfortable, but a wedding's main contributing factor is the open bar. Another factor is what I call "Wedding Envy." Most women love the idea of getting married and the whole experience gets them wrapped up in the moment, which in turn, makes you a potential target. So…mix free alcohol, with the romance of a wedding and throw in a dance floor… and once again, it's game time!

5. **Small Towns:**

Oh yes! The good ol' small town girls! They are always surprisingly hot and surprisingly ready to get down. If you're a big city boy like me, there's nothing better than going to a small bar/club in a small town. Since all the girls know every local within a fifty-mile radius, a relatively attractive new man is like Joe Montana with the football…touchdown! In a small town, you're on the receiving end, all you have to do is catch the ball and run with it. How many yards you gain all depends on how well you move your feet!

The 70

The Rules of the Game

This is it fellas, the core of the book. Ninety percent of what I've said so far has no bearing if you don't read and follow this chapter. If you were allowed only one chapter to read, this would be it. Most people wouldn't even disclose the information I'm about to tell you, but we're on the same team now, so listen up!

In the next few pages, I've broken down what I feel is the 10 most important Rules of the Game. When it comes to top gun training, this chapter would be it!

Let's get inverted.

ROE MODEL: KATHRYN SMITH

RULE # 1:

You Must Engage!

Hesitation is not an option! In football, when you receive the kickoff, if you just stand there, you'll certainly be laid-out. It's similar in dating, everyone has ball carrying opportunities, but if you hesitate, the good plays will just pass you by. Winners want the ball!

We have all been there… standing in line somewhere next to a hot girl searching for the words, but couldn't muster up the courage to say anything. What a wasted opportunity! You don't have to be annoying about it, but if you feel anything at all, you owe it to yourself to at least try. Remember, worse-case scenario, she blows you off! Oh well, you'll be exactly where you are now... arms crossed, quietly kicking yourself in the ass.

Let's consider this real world example:

Imagine you step up to a "Bar" and look right and see a beautiful girl standing next to you. Like a reflex, you must say something. If you wait even a few seconds, uncomfortable silence will sink in and you'll have no chance. This type of response/reflex takes practice. If you're shy, warm up on some less intimidating girls so

41

you're ready when your big chance comes.

There's a funny thing about girls, they can feel our presence the moment we walk up. If you're unconfident and searching for the words, you might as well just stick a fork in your ass, 'cause your done! Remember, it's better to have engaged and scared off a perfectly good "bogie," than to have never engaged at all!

Now...how to engage is a whole different story. The great thing about this rule is that it's somewhat pre-meditated. Pick-up lines are "OUT." But witty banter is like Robert Horry's 3-point shot at the buzzer... Money!!! With practice, you'll learn how to key into any situation and turn it into an opening line. Just try and find something currently happening by surveying the scene or eaves drop on a conversation. Once you have laid one out there and she bites, the barrier has been broken and now you're just working down the field. Let's run another example but fill in some dialogue to get the ideas flowing:

Example:
(Hot girl in supermarket appears from behind a cloud)
There you are standing in line to pay for groceries when you notice a smoking hot girl out of the corner of your eye. First thing to do is quickly survey the scene. Scan magazines, her cart, your cart...any similarities? Make sure to also scan for a wedding ring or Tiffany's

bracelet. These are dead giveaways you'll be turned down.

If all is clear, knock away…
"Hey, I see you have my favorite ice cream!"

This will hopefully start a conversation.

The point is to get something going. Just make sure it seems non-premeditated and avoid any pickup lines. Remember, she is expecting those and she'll raise her defense. If you can get in a few exchanged sentences, that's called conversation and by the time you realize what's happened, you'll be asking for her number!

Remember, even if she blows you off, be happy that you engaged because it makes for good practice. Secondly, you'll feel good you manned up and talked to a cute girl.

Summary

Rule #1:

1. Don't hesitate! Learn to react unconsciously.

2. No cheesy pickup lines.

3. Survey the scene and find witty conversation starters.

Rule # 2:

Don't Bitch Out!

Ahhhh yes…This one is good! My brother and friends came up with this one recently, and we have been field-testing it ever since. I've moved it to Rule Number 2 because it has been extremely successful.

What we have noticed is that girls tend to check us out more than we think they do! Eye contact is how they show interest. We discovered that men tend to look away. I don't know why, we just do. I assume it's because we don't want girls to think we're staring… but ironically, it has a reverse effect! What has really happened is… "YOU BITCHED OUT!" She stared at you to get your attention and you looked away like a bitch. What you need to do is grab your nuts and not look away. If you can look someone in the eye, it's the same as saying hello. The longer the better! When she is looking at you, she's thinking:

First few moments, "Oh he's cute…"
Next few moments, "Oh hold up, he's not bitchin' out…"
Couple moments after that, "Hey now… what's up with this guy, do I know him?"

45

Closing moments, "Oh, it's on, get over here and talk to me."

After a "Don't Bitch Out" engagement, talking to the girl is easy. It's like you already know her.

Now, just to be clear, I'm not saying you should go staring every girl down like you're John Wayne. I'm just stating that, if you happen to make eye contact with a girl, give it a couple moments. Test out this rule, you're going to laugh at how many times you've been bitchin' out!

Summary

Rule #2:

1. **If you catch a girl looking at you, not looking away shows your self-confidence.**

2. **Don't stare down girls like John Wayne. This only applies when a girl is checking you out.**

Rule # 3:

Lets After-Party!

When I was 21, I was fearless and so were most of my friends. We would wear the loudest shirts and made sure people knew we were there. Looking back on the whole thing makes me laugh! But…the one thing us young bucks always had energy for, was a good ol' fashion after-party!

Back then; we always pushed for the after-party! In fact, we wouldn't even take no for an answer. Shit, two o'clock was early and it was expected! As I got older, I'm not sure why, I stopped asking. Recently reflecting on why things weren't as good as the old days, I realized that Rule Number 3 had been abandoned. Therefore, I've been pushing the after party again and have been surprised on its success. If you can get a group of girls to come back to the house…it's, as my friend Justin would say, "go time!"

Now, when you ask a girl, it should be in the form of a statement, not a question.

For Example:

"Grab your girls. We're headed to my friends after-party!"

Don't give her the opportunity to rationalize and reject. Girls have grown up with all kinds of rules telling them what they should and should not do. Trust me when I say, she wants to be crazy. She has been dancing with you all night, so keeping the party going is natural. If all your boys are doing their jobs right, this should be a slam-dunk. If she insists "No" - no big deal! You tried…missed…and now it's time to resort immediately to Rule #4.

Summary

Rule #3:

1. **When the bar is closing, always remember to suggest an after-party.**

2. **If she says no, make sure you get her number for another night! Rule Number 4.**

Rule # 4:

Get Her Number!

Let's say you've had a good night. You've logged forty some minutes of conversation, have at least two drinks invested, and your undershirt is damp from dancing! At this point, the only mistake you could make is to not get her number! I know this seems obvious, but all kinds of circumstances can and do happen. "I didn't save it correctly," "I gave her my number," whatever! If I were a betting man (which I am), odds are slim to none that you'll ever see her again and slim left with a girl an hour ago. In the course of writing this book, I've even shanked a few myself. Below is a recent example:

My Shank Example (FORE!):

I was in Las Vegas. I met a girl in a bar called, "The Beach." We danced, drank, talked until the sunrise… we completely connected and so far I was really into her. When it was closing time, 6 a.m., I didn't have my cell on me, so I gave my number to her and we made arrangements to take a nap and meet in the afternoon. Now, the good news is she called, the bad news is I couldn't understand her voice mail and no incoming caller ID was on my phone...I never heard from her again! "Good one – D."

This is a classic example of getting too cocky. I was sure we'd find each other, but c'mon...it's Vegas! What I should have done is gone old fashion and found a napkin and pen. That way I, for sure, would have her number.

Below is another flagrant example of poor athleticism.

Another Example (Bad Form!):

I had a work buddy of mine come out with me to a new club in Hollywood. He was new to the scene, and I wanted to show him a good time. He is extremely shy, but good-looking and super smart. His usual nights consisted of reading or researching the web. I told him it was time to go out and I wanted him to run a few "down and outs" or maybe even go deep for a touchdown. So, off we went! At the club, we saw two girls talking outside. He was shocked on how easy it was to move over and open a conversation. Even I was a little shocked, it was **textbook**!

All the rules applied. It was like he was a veteran, and we each picked one to talk to. We spent thirty-some minutes shooting the shit and it turns out that his girl was a Chemical Engineer, hot and smart...go figure! We eventually took a break and did a few **laps** around the bar. We didn't see his girl again until it was time to leave. So here we are… last call and working our way out. All of sudden, there she is, five steps in front of me, the Chemical Engineer.

We made eye contact and she said, "Where have you guys been? I've been looking for you." I smiled as she gazed at my friend. Knowing my place and being a good wingman, I stepped aside to let me friend engage and close. To my surprise, he said "bye" and caught up with me. My mouth dropped open, I said "What the fuck! Did you get her number?" He replied, "No, I didn't think of it." It took me a minute to calm down. I glanced back only to see another guy getting her number. It was too late!

He was so bummed on the whole car ride home that I made him practice:
"I had a really good time talking with you.
I would love to hang out again…Can I get your number?"

He must have said it twenty-five times and we still joke about it.

Moral is…girls rarely call guys! No matter what the excuse, always get her number. Put it in your phone, write it down, get a card, anything! Just make sure you have it and it's clear with no mistakes. That's the law of the land, obey it!

Summary

Rule #4:

1. Always take her number!

2. Don't rush while saving or writing down her number, a mistake here will cost you.

Rule # 5:

Get Yourself a Wingman or Two!

Ok, it's Friday night and you're going out. Wallet… check, ID…check, Wingmen…check-check. In this day and age, if you're a single man going out, it's imperative you never leave home without your Wingman, or even better, a whole squad of Wingmen. There is even a new phenomenon of wingwomen. Whatever the case, going out is always more fun with friends. Any man that rolls solo to the bars is bordering desperate and remember, girls can smell that shit like dogs can smell fear. More importantly, nine times out of ten, you'll meet a group of two or more girls and you'll be out numbered. Unless you're an amazing Pilot, when you're out numbered, odds are you'll be shot down.

When you're with your wingmen, there is nothing more fun than discussing battle strategies at the bar. Even if you don't make a kill, you still can buzz that tower a few times and laugh about some good combat stories. The key is to have fun and not try so hard. You will be surprised on how "Just Having Fun" increases the attractive appearance of the group. There's an interesting thing about girls and their sixth sense, a carefree and fun group is like a magnet. Girls notice these guys and are attracted to it.

When it comes to selecting wingmen, it's important to consider the strengths and weaknesses of each of your crew. Not always is the good looking guy your best choice. Some guys make horrible Wingmen, some are selfish and like to break off and engage solo, some are boring and the girl they pair off with loses interest and bugs out. Let me remind you, she will circle around and eventually shoot you and your squad down. It will happen so fast you'll be quoting lines from *Top Gun* – "Where'd she goooooo…Where'd who goooo!"

The rule of thumb is, pick guys that compliment the group. A funny guy is a strong asset. Also, watch out for "I" guys, they are not team players and will not work in formation.

So, now that you have good Pilots, check your gear and get your squad off the flight deck!

Summary

Rule #5:

1. Choose good Wingmen who are happy to see you hook up! Watch out for the "I" guy.

2. Go out with the intention of having fun. "Just having fun" is attractive to the oppisite sex.

ROE MODEL: TIFFANY LANG

56

Rule # 6:

Divide and Conquer!

Like I said earlier, when it comes to going out, women's "mentality" is much different than ours. Women are looking to have fun, get wild, and party with their friends! While we, on the other hand, are looking to have fun, get wild, and SCORE! Imagine for a moment being a woman. You decide whether you want to "hook up" or not. If you decide you do…it will certainly happen! Knowing this makes the whole idea of "hooking-up" less appealing. It's easy, and therefore, not as big a deal. Worse yet, as a girl, if you do go out on a limb and do something like "have sex," it's frowned upon. Doesn't that just suck!

Men, on the other hand, get "high-fives" for each woman they land and therefore are rewarded for the accomplishment. This fundamental difference is the key reason why women make the decision in the "hooking up" department. Therefore, the only chance we have of breaking the norm is to effectively "Divide and Conquer!"

Now, what the hell is "Divide and Conquer?"

I've just illustrated why women are cautious around their friends. When girls are together in an environment like a bar or club, they're more likely to "dog you" and save their reputation. The exception is if you're really good looking and they've gotten the green light from their friends. More often, hooking up is not their main objective. Would you believe they actually came to dance?

Now, there are those cases when a woman, or even group of women, have recently become single or have had a day where they feel "un-sexy." In these cases, all they can think of doing is finding the biggest "bad-boy" in the place and use him as a toy. Good news is, us "toys" love it! Bad news is, nights like these are few and far between and it's a better bet to rely on some advanced maneuvering like the "Divide and Conquer."

So without further procrastination, let me explain the maneuver:

Your chances are always quadrupled if you and the boys can evenly divide a group of girls so they're one on one. Once one on one, you take out the reputation element and your girl will let her guard down just enough to get to know you. The tricky part is, you have to make sure it's an even ratio. If you leave even one girl in the group flying solo, she will circle around, gather her friends and call off the attack (better known as the phase, "We were salted by the **grenade**").

The concept is simple! If you're a group of four guys, you need to seek out a group of four girls. Amazingly enough, this somehow happens more times than none! If you need to, call in reinforcements by launching the guys you have on **ready five**. Whatever the case, you must even those odds!

To recap, this technical maneuver requires skilled work from not only you, but also your squad. There are all kinds of things that can and do go wrong, but with good tactics and fair rotation on who **dives on the grenade** (Rule #7), all the boys can have fun.

Summary

Rule #6:

1. When you're out with the
    boys, find a group of girls
    with an even ratio.

2. Never alienate a girl in the
    other group. She will circle
    around and steal the other
    girls from you and your
    Wingmen.

Rule # 7:

Diving on the Grenade!

This rule is important no matter if you're fat, skinny, short, tall, or super good looking. It's every comrade's duty to his fellow soldiers to **dive on the grenade**.

More popularly known as "Taking one for the team," it's been an unwritten tradition since the dawn of "I could remember." On a scale of one to ten, most girls you meet aren't going to have a group average of nine or ten. More likely, it will be an average of five or six and there's always ONE who's just not into the scene (not having fun, not attractive, doesn't get enough attention, whatever!). So, it's going to take the efforts of all the boys to entertain the group, even the **grenade**, so at least one or two lucky men go home smiling!

Like I explained earlier, if you leave even just one girl abandoned, she will circle around and convince all the girls to bolt. I've seen it happen too many times to count.

Friend: "Diesel… what happened to that girl you were with?"

61

Diesel: "Salted by the ugly friend, yet once again!"

In some cases, you take matters into your own hands and dive on that puppy yourself. But don't worry, all you have to do is run interference for a few hours while your teammates run off a few good plays. Dance, drink, tell jokes…you know, be an "all around fun guy." Some ringers even go the extra distance and "hook up." I can't blame them either, a man's godda do, what a man's godda do. I'll admit, to my friends, I'm considered one of the best **grenade-men** in the business. It's nothing to be ashamed of, and in the eyes of your friends, you should be a damn hero.

In the morning, if for some reason, your friends decide to "bag" on you, then they're not your friends. They should thank you; buy you breakfast and next time around take dibs on the **grenade** themselves.

Cardinal rule…your boys must rotate being the **grenade** man. If one of the boys is selfish and not pulling his weight, he doesn't deserve to be up on the front line with the rest of you!

Summary

Rule #7:

1. Never leave a girl in the group solo. She will get bored and take all the girls out of the game.

2. Boys must rotate being the "Grenade Man." Watch out for "I" guys who don't fall into rank and pull their weight.

ROE MODEL: CAMILLE ANDERSON

Rule # 8:

Pity is for the Weak!

Oh poor you. You've just broken up with your girlfriend or haven't been very lucky with the ladies lately. Well, get over it! While you're moping, you're pissing away good opportunities! Hate to break it to you, but, it's the same story for all of us, including women. Dating is one of the hardest games in the world and just because you're on a losing streak doesn't entitle you to the next win.

I've seen it too many times to count, a guy on a first date belting out his love problems. "It always seems to slip out" they say. Just because a girl seems sympathetic to your problems and the conversation appears to be connecting your new relationship, in the long run, she'll never really respect you. You'll always be "that guy" that someone else didn't want. Why would you want to tell the other team about your weaknesses? It's never a good way to start the ball game. More important, it gives your date a negative view of yourself. Remember what I said was the most sought after quality in men, confidence. At this point, you look like nothing more than an un-eaten hot dog at the end of the grill, "Just one big dried-out weenie."

While on the sideline, I always like to reverse my thinking. Try to think of a girl you've gone out with that seemed desperate. When her entire happiness seems to be riding on you "liking" her, it tends to be a turn-off rather than a turn-on. It's too much pressure early in the relationship. Nobody's ready for that kind of commitment on the first date!

"So Diesel… what am I suppose to talk about?"

"Anything but the weather!"

The best thing to do is listen! Listening is a very powerful quality most men are really bad at. If you can learn good listening skills, you'll find it much easier to get to know someone. When you do speak, stick to the positive things in your life. Don't try to be someone you're not. If you're passionate about computers, but think it may be "nerd-like" conversation, you're wrong! That's who you are, and what you're most comfortable talking about. Who knows, she may be a computer nut as well! More importantly, talking about your passions is what makes you comfortable and therefore appear more confident. On a first date, that's exactly where you want to be!

My best example is a buddy of mine who is relatively new to the dating circuit. He's by far the most talented and smart programmer I know. But when it comes to dating, he's about as green as the "Patron Silver" label. He recently told me an interesting story about his last "Yahoo" date. He said he tried to stay away from any "Shoptalk." But as the date progressed, he felt as though he had nothing to talk about and she seemed bored. While he and I reflected about his date, he claimed he felt ordinary. I was partly responsible because earlier in the week, I told him to stay away from any computer shit, "you may lose her in technology." I quickly realized I was wrong, but before I could say anything he completely surprises me with an independent comment. He told me, "Going forward, I'm going to talk about what I do because that's who I am, and if my date doesn't like it, oh well!"

I had the biggest smile on my face because I realized he just uncovered the big secret. He was happy and proud of himself. At that moment, he didn't seem like the naive guy anymore, he seemed confident and ready for his next date. I told him I had made a mistake, and I couldn't have agreed with him more!

What I learned from this experience is the person we will most likely end up falling in love with, will look at our accomplishments and consider them a turn-on!

In conclusion, Rule #8 is all about our initial perception. If you don't have confidence in yourself, you won't find it in the arms of your first date. Stay away from talking about your past relationships and don't avoid who you are. Also, on a first date, your most powerful tool is to shut up and listen! Many men tend to talk more than they listen, some even cut people off. It's immature and gets you nowhere. When listening, don't be afraid to look her straight in the eyes. Many of us look down or away and it's a dead giveaway of our insecurities. Staring someone in the eyes is very personal and attractive.

Summary

Rule #8:

1. **Never talk about your past relationships on a first date. It just leads to ordinary conversation.**

2. **Don't be someone you're not, lying makes you look uncomfortable and insecure.**

3. **Try to listen more than you talk. You don't need to prove yourself in an hour.**

Rule # 9:

Hit the Beach Strong!

In every successful battle strategy, the aggressor stormed the beach with overwhelming force and fury. Now getting the girl shouldn't be like blazing down the enemy, but a confident group of men that go out in force, and look like they're having fun…attract women. Try this little experiment: Next time you're out, scan the room and take a minute to survey the scene. Without being gay, pay close attention to the different types of men. First you'll see the group of guys looking so hard for girls it's just straight embarrassing (don't be those guys). Next you'll see a group of guys who are laughing and joking around. They're having fun and appear to be in a world of their own. Log that in, because later, you'll see that same group of guys all pair off with ladies on the dance floor. It's like a fuckin' science, I swear!

The secret is not really that complicated. Girls are attracted to guys who look like they're having fun. The trick is, as strange as it may sounds, while looking for girls, you have to act as though you're not looking for girls. It's like…"Hello I see the enemy in the bushes, but I'm going to pretend I don't, and then flank them

69

from the left." Don't worry, girls are quick and will notice your group. You're not going to lose them by 9:30pm. Be patient and it will happen.

The Group Mindset

The group mindset is the driving force behind the term "Hit the Beach Strong." Your group needs to appear confident and powerful so the enemy will just surrender without a fight. The trick is, how do you setup a positive group mindset? Good question… below is a quick example of what you can do to prepare for battle.

Before you go out, like in the car ride or while pre-partying, pump up the group. Tell them how "money" they are, trade stories from prior weekends and loosen everyone up. These stories not only bond your group, they build confidence and excitement for the night to come. Secondly, everyone, including men, enjoy compliments! It's not gay to tell your friend he's got on a good looking shirt. It's a good way to start the night, and if he's pumped, it's better for the group mindset.

Summary

Rule #9:

1. Girls are attracted to a group that looks fun.

2. Make sure your group is not looking for ladies while out LOOKING for ladies. That's the underlying objective. Don't make it obvious.

3. Pre-party and pump up your crew before you get out to the bar.

ROE MODEL: MICHELLE MARIE

Rule # 10:

Organize Even Odds!

Rule Number 10 is all about even odds. This is probably the only time you can use the two words together and get away with it. Some of my most memorable times have been when the boys and I organized a night with an even ratio of girls. Like in any game, both teams must have the same number of players. If the other team has one extra, you won't be able to defend everyone and probably lose. Inversely, if you have one too many, one of you will be rolling solo and hating life.

The tricky part is not playing the game, it's getting enough players to play a night game in the first place!

Let's run through a quick game-organizing scenario:

Let's say you call up "Lisa" who you met last week at the beach.

"Lisa, it's me. Met you last week… yeah… how are you… cool… listen, my boys and I are going out tonight. Can you round up three friends and join us?"

Lisa will claim that her girls already have plans, but here is where rookies fail and you'll succeed. Giving up is not an option!

"Lisa, you'll have way more fun if you come with us. How many girls are you with tonight?"

The key is to immediate follow with the "how many" question like it's already happening. Once you get "Lisa" to agree, the hard part is over.

Once out, have fun, don't smother, and let the game take its course. Remember to resort to the earlier rules to make the night a complete success. If you've forgotten already, lets review.

Start earlier in the afternoon with Rule #6 – Get yourself some wingmen. Once selected, get the boys over early enough to pre-party and enforce Rule #9 – Hit the beach strong, which will get them pumped about the game. Once out, remind the boys to engage (Rule #1) followed by Rule #7 – Divide and conquer. #7 should be natural to any good team. Toward the end of the night, call in Rule #2 – Lets After Party. A couple drinking games at the house and then, as the wee hours creep up, people should be paired off and comfortable. One of your friends will be on the grenade, and he'll be the one getting a free breakfast.

You, if you did your job right, will be with Lisa… who, may I remind you, is the one you liked in the first place.

The final step is for everyone to remember that when it's time to split, put Rule #4 into action and get numbers. There is more fun left in this group! Hell, maybe one of these girls could really turn out to be the one you've always been looking for, but that's for a whole different book entirely. Have fun!

Summary

Rule #10:

1. When going out with a group of girls, make sure the ratios are even.

2. Select a good group of Wingmen. One bad Pilot can take out the entire squad.
3. Remember your training and the rules of game.

The 80

Hand Signals (with illustrations)

The good ol' "Ejection handle," or maybe you want to signal for a "lap." Every good team communicates without speaking. I encourage you to use, modify, and create your own customized hand signals for your squad. Here are a few the boys and I use on the field:

The Eject Signal

Ok, you've had a few drinks and according to the beer goggles you're wearing, the girl you're sitting with is HOT! Then, out of the corner of your eye, you see one of your boys giving you **the eject signal**. This means it's time to exit. Always trust your Wingman, maybe you've had a few too many or he has better options. Whatever the reason, when your wingman tells you to eject…reach back and pull the handle!

The Eye Brow Rub

There are always times when you need a little backup. Whether it's a Wingman for "the friend", or you need a good exit strategy, **the eye brow rub** is the universal signal that means you need help! The great thing about this signal is no one will ever question you about on it, even though our eyebrows never really itch!

Let's Do a Lap

There you are with your buddy standing by the bar. The place is starting to fill up and the two Long Islands you've had are starting to kick in. Now is a good time to signal for a **lap**. This signal is the universal question, "Do you want to take a look around the bar with me?"

Bogies on my Six

You glance around the room and see a group of hot ladies behind you. The "OLD YOU" would have tapped your friend on the shoulder and pointed, which would have most definitely got you **picked off**. Here's a safe way you can use to inform your wingman of bogies in the area. Point to your eyes and then tell your friend, **bogies on my six**. This one can be used with any direction; **bogies on my nine, bogies twelve o'clock**, etc.

Clipped

This one is pretty self-explanatory. If you've stopped dating a girl and your friend asks about her, show him the scissors and cut. She's been **clipped**!

Grenade

Pull the pin before you throw this one! This is how you signal that you think the girl you're paired off with fits the description of the **grenade**. Vice versa, your friends can use this one to signal for help.

I'm Out Dawg!

Maybe it's a bad scene, or you just want to try another club. Whatever the reason, when it's time to go, there's no better exit than the classic casino **I'm out dawg**. Adapted from untrusting casinos owners who require that dealers show their hands to the cameras before exiting, throw out this sign and start for the door, because your friends will know… "You're out!"

The 90

Flipping the Script
(Pulling out a win in a losing situation.)

I hate to admit it, but every man, even the best of us, get in situations where we lose our edge. I wish I could say it was easy to find a relationship where both parties are equally into each other, but most of the time it's either one or the other. Sometimes you'll be the coveted one, but most of the time it's reversed. This situation can be extremely frustrating because no matter how hard you try, nothing seems to work! To be frank, you should start accepting your losses because when a mind is made up, odds are slim you'll bring it back! With that said, let's continue.

Just because a team seems like it has no chance of winning, doesn't mean all the players should walk off the field. So what does any good coach do in these situations?

"Accept his losses and call for a "Hail Mary." You never know…it may score the game winning touchdown."

Below are three "Hail Mary" plays you can try in the final minutes of the game. The key word is final! If you randomly throw out these plays and the game has been over for 3 weeks, don't think they'll work! You'll be playing when everyone has gone home, and the field is empty. Only try these on girls you've recently lost to the dark side.

Hail Mary Play #1. "The Take Away"

Pretty straightforward. You take away what you currently offer. For example, if you are the one who always calls, call 1/4 as much, or if you have the balls, not at all! Wait for her to call. If she does, the extra point is good!

I know this sounds strange "Why would you not call a girl you like?" Simple…by not calling, she'll wonder why you've stopped calling. Then wonder will turn into curiosity. Pretty soon, she'll be messing with her own head and it won't be about you anymore. It'll be about her, and why you're not calling. This doesn't always work, but if it does, you have successfully extended the game into overtime.

Hail Mary Play #2. "No Huddle Offense"

If "The Take Away" doesn't work, one of your only other options is a high risk play called, "No Huddle

Offense." This is where you become very persistent and throw out play after play without rest. Sometimes this persistent offense can wear down her defense and lower her guard. Timing is everything and while running this play, you should check in every couple days. Sometimes give it a week, but stay in touch by calling, text messaging, or emailing. Of course, never call twice in the same day, and if you've called three times with no response, give it a rest!

Otherwise, if she does communicate with you, after a while, you may flip the script and she'll be the one contacting you!

The one major problem with this "Hail Mary" technique is that you risk looking like a total and utter tool. You could lose big points and hurt your stats. But, if you really, really like the girl and want to give it one more hoorah, then give this a try. Just be careful and if you see any sign of annoyance, peel off and save face.

Hail Mary Play #3. "The Decoy"
This last play is a lot lower on the scale when it comes to smooth and crafty. This one is just down right sneaky. But, desperate times call for desperate measures! Nothing pisses off a girl more than you dating her friend. Girls talk all the time and when she hears all the wonderful things you're doing for the friend, she'll second-guess herself. With this play, you

run the risk of the friend really liking you, or worse, you fumble and mess it up with the whole group. But in some small cases, you can call this play and actually make a catch. Sometimes the original girl will pull you aside at some party and start flirting with you because you've been such a good date to her friend. When that opportunity arises, do what your heart tells you.

A Big Footnote:
In conclusion, most of these plays are "Hail Mary's." It will only be sheer luck that you catch the ball in the end zone. So don't consider these anything worth using on a regular basis. When the game is over, it's usually over! Best thing to do is go run some bleachers and prepare for the next game.

Touchdown!

Throughout our history, men have had visions. Thomas Edison saw a nation of electricity, Bill Gates saw a nation of personal PC's…I, see a nation of men going home with hot ladies and a big smile!

Although this is the end of the book, as cheesy as this may sound, it's really only the beginning. It's important you understand this because you're now part of my vision. When you think of the Rules of Engagement "ROE," I don't want you to think of a self-help book you've read. I want you to reflect on a new way of looking at your social life. I want you to analyze the game and have general understanding of what works and what doesn't. I want you to make better decisions on a date and have lasting memories with your friends.

Most of all, I want you not to add to the predictable stereotype we men have created. It's time to live in this new and exciting lifestyle…the attitude of the 21st century man who believes in himself, enjoys his job, his friends, and his social life. It's also a man who is more sophisticated in dating.

To fit the profile, you don't have to be the guy who lands tons of girls. On the contrary, it's more about the guy that girls want to hang with. The guy or group of guys' that girls consider fun!

There's been this myth that "Girls love Assholes!" Actually, it's more that girls love a man who's funny, confident, witty, and makes them feel comfortable. Nowhere in that list of characteristics is "Asshole." That's just something men have derived because of a lack of understanding.

That guy walking with those hot girls may be an asshole to you, but to the girls, he's charming, funny, witty and self-confident.

Recently a friend asked me, "Diesel, what's this Rules of Engagement book all about…is it some sort of book on how to land chicks?" I told him, "No, there is no book on how to do that!

Rules of Engagement won't help you score with a girl in seven easy steps. It's a reminder that dating is fun and the journey is what prepares us for the rest of our lives. It's a reminder that your self-esteem and happiness depends on you and not the actions of others. It's the attitude of a man who takes responsibility for his actions and control of his life.

There's a funny thing about the way our physiological minds work. Sometimes the less you try and force something, the better off it goes. If any of you've played golf, you'd know exactly what I mean. The more you relax your swing, the straighter and further that damn little ball goes! I've found this compares to dating as well. The more patient and calm you are, the more successful you become. Even though this book only focuses on the social part, I believe this philosophy trickles down to every aspect of our lives.

Be careful on how you take this advice. By no means am I saying you should be lazy and good fortune will find you. I'm just stating the obvious…focus on what you can control, like your job, your actions and your accomplishments. Don't sweat the little stuff and it will all fall into place.

With that said, I want you to start your "ROE" life. Visit the roelife.com website, check out the beautiful "ROE" Models, hell…buy a "Grenade Man" t-shirt. Keep your eye out for upcoming events, products, and programming. Don't forget your rules and try not to fumble the ball on the 1-yard line. I'll see you out on the field. Good Luck!

Diesel